Everyman's Poetry

Everyman, I will go with thee,
and be thy guide

Shall I compare thee to a summer's day?

Shakespeare's Love Poetry

Selected and edited by A. D. P. BRIGGS
University of Birmingham

EVERYMAN
J. M. Dent · London

This edition first published by Everyman Paperbacks in 1999
Selection, introduction and other critical apparatus
© J. M. Dent 1999

J. M. Dent
Orion Publishing Group
Orion House
5 Upper St Martin's Lane
London WC2H 9EA

Typeset by Deltatype Ltd, Birkenhead, Merseyside
Printed in Great Britain by
The Guernsey Press Co. Ltd, Guernsey, C.I.

British Library Cataloguing-in-Publication
Data is available on request

ISBN 0 460 88207 4

Contents

Note on the Author and Editor

WILLIAM SHAKESPEARE is held to have been born on St George's Day, 23 April 1564. The eldest son of a prosperous glove-maker in Stratford-upon-Avon, he was probably educated at the town's grammar school.

Tradition holds that between 1585 and 1592, Shakespeare first became a schoolteacher and then set off for London. By 1595 he was a leading member of the Lord Chamberlain's Men, helping to direct their business affairs, as well as being a playwright and actor. In 1598 he became a part-owner of the company, which was the most distinguished of its age. However, he maintained his contacts with Stratford, and his family seem to have remained there.

From about 1610 he seems to have grown increasingly involved in the town's affairs, suggesting a withdrawal from London. He died on 23 April 1616, on his fifty-second birthday, and was buried at Holy Trinity Church two days later.

A. D. P. BRIGGS, Professor of Russian Language and Literature at the University of Birmingham, is a specialist in modern Russian literature, mainly of the nineteenth century, and European poetry. Among his many publications are ten books, five of them devoted to Alexander Pushkin. His editions of Pushkin and FitzGerald's *Omar Khayyám* have already appeared in the Everyman's Poetry series.

Chronology of Shakespeare's Life

Year[1]	Age	Life
1564		Shakespeare baptised 26 April at Stratford-upon-Avon
1582	18	Marries Anne Hathaway
1583	19	Daughter, Susanna, born
1585	21	Twin son and daughter, Hamnet and Judith, born
1590–1	26	*The Two Gentlemen of Verona & The Taming of the Shrew*
1591	27	*2 & 3 Henry VI*
1592	28	*Titus Andronicus & I Henry VI*
1592–3		*Richard III*
1593	29	*Venus and Adonis* published
1594	30	*The Comedy of Errors. The Rape of Lucrece* published
1594–5		*Love's Labour's Lost*

Chronology of his Times

Year	Artistic Events	Historical Events
1565–7	Golding, Ovid's *Metamorphoses*, tr.	Elizabeth I reigning
1574	*A Mirror for Magistrates* (3rd ed.)	
1576	London's first playhouse built	
1578	John Lyly, *Euphues*	
1579	North, Plutarch's *Lives*, tr. Spenser, *Shepheardes Calender*	
1587	Marlowe, *I Tamburlaine* Holinshed's *Chronicles* (2nd ed.)	Mary Queen of Scots executed Defeat of Spanish Armada
1589	Kyd, *Spanish Tragedy* Marlowe, *Jew of Malta*	Civil war in France
1590	Spenser, *Faerie Queene*, Bks I–III	
1591	Sidney, *Astrophil and Stella*	Proclamation against Jesuits
1592	Marlowe, *Dr Faustus & Edward II*	Scottish witchcraft trials Plague closes theatres from June
1593	Marlowe killed	
1594	Nashe, *Unfortunate Traveller*	Theatres reopen in summer
1594–6		Extreme food shortages

Year[1]	Age	Life
1595	31	*A Midsummer Night's Dream, Romeo and Juliet & Richard II.* An established member of Lord Chamberlain's Men
1596	32	*King John.* Hamnet dies
1596–7		*The Merchant of Venice & 1 Henry IV*
1597	33	Buys New Place in Stratford
		The Lord Chamberlain's Men's lease to play at the Theatre expires; until 1599 they play mainly at the Curtain
1597–8		*The Merry Wives of Windsor & 2 Henry IV*
1598	34	*Much Ado About Nothing*
1598–9		*Henry V*
1599	35	*Julius Caesar.* One of the syndicate responsible for building the Globe in Southwark, where the Lord Chamberlain's Men now play
1599–1600		*As You Like It*
1600–1		*Hamlet*
1601	37	*Twelfth Night.* His father is buried in Stratford
1602	38	*Troilus and Cressida.* Invests £320 in land near Stratford[2]
1603	39	*Measure for Measure.* The Lord Chamberlain's Men become the King's Men. They play at court more than all the other companies combined
1603–4		*Othello*
c. 1604	40	Shakespeare sues Philip Rogers of Stratford for debt
1604–5		*All's Well that Ends Well*
1605	41	*Timon of Athens.* Invests £440 in Stratford tithes
1605–6		*King Lear*
1606	42	*Macbeth & Antony and Cleopatra*

Year	Artistic Events	Historical Events
1595	Sidney, *An Apologie for Poetry*	Riots in London
1596		Calais captured by Spanish Cádiz expedition
1597	Bacon's *Essays*	
1598	Marlowe and Chapman, *Hero and Leander* Jonson, *Every Man in his Humour*	Rebellion in Ireland
1599	Children's companies begin playing Thomas Dekker's *Shoemaker's Holiday*	Essex fails in Ireland
1601	'War of the Theatres' Jonson, *Poetaster*	Essex rebels and is executed
1602		Tyrone defeated in Ireland
1603	Florio, Montaigne's *Essays*, tr.	Elizabeth I dies, James I accedes Raleigh found guilty of treason
1604	Marston, *The Malcontent*	Peace with Spain
1605	Bacon's *Advancement of Learning*	Gunpowder plot
1606	Jonson's *Volpone*	

Year[1]	Age	Life
1607	43	*Pericles.* Susanna marries the physician John Hall in Stratford
1608	44	*Coriolanus.* The King's Men lease Blackfriars, an indoor theatre. His only grandchild is born. His mother dies
1609	45	*The Winter's Tale.* 'Sonnets' and 'A Lover's Complaint' published
1610	46	*Cymbeline*
1611	47	*The Tempest*
1613	49	*Henry VIII.* Buys house in London for £140
1613–4		*The Two Noble Kinsmen*
1616	52	Judith marries Thomas Quiney, a vintner, in Stratford. On 23 April he dies, and is buried two days later
1623		Publication of the First Folio. His wife dies in August

[1] It is rarely possible to be certain about the dates at which plays of this period were written. For Shakespeare's plays, this chronology follows the dates preferred by Wells and Taylor, the editors of the Oxford Shakespeare. Publication dates are given for poetry and books.

[2] A schoolmaster would earn around £20 a year at this time.

Year	Artistic Events	Historical Events
1607	Tourneur's *The Revenger's Tragedy* published	Virginia colonised Enclosure riots
1609		Oath of allegiance Truce in Netherlands
1610	Jonson, *Alchemist*	
1611	Authorized Version of the Bible Donne, *Anatomy of the World*	
1612	Webster, *White Devil*	Prince Henry dies
1613	Webster, *Duchess of Malfi*	Princess Elizabeth marries
1614	Jonson, *Bartholomew Fair*	
1616	Folio edition of Jonson's plays	

Biographical note and chronology compiled by John Lee, University of Bristol, 1993.

Introduction

This senior-junior, giant-dwarf, Dan Cupid

Love's Labour's Lost

William Shakespeare, our national poet, commonly described as the world's greatest writer, has left us an inexhaustible fund of ideas. His works treats every subject, from the most trivial to the most sublime, but his persistent preoccupation is with Love. This theme runs throughout his work, figuring strongly in most of the plays and dominating many. His other works, the sonnets and various poems, are all about erotic relationships of one kind or another.

You will find in Shakespeare a hundred definitions of Love (but no single one for all purposes) and a Love quotation for every occasion. The urgency, the variety and the contradictions of the subject are depicted with relish, humour, delight and despair. Love is a mighty lord or a blind fool, a cruel master or a 'wimpled, whining, purblind, wayward boy'. Love, the enemy of reason, otherwise a fever, a devil or an evil angel, reappears elsewhere as a guiding star, an uplifting force that will take you to sing hymns at heaven's gate.

The Sonnets

A sonnet was originally a love poem by definition, so that all of Shakespeare's sonnets necessarily deal with this topic. There are 154 of them, written probably between 1593 and 1601, and they were published in 1609, with a dedication to a mysterious 'Mr W.H.', possibly the young Earl of Southampton. Most of them appear to have been addressed to a young man rather than a woman, and this includes perhaps the most famous of them all, 'Shall I compare thee to a summer's day?' (18). Unanswerable questions swarm around them. Were they predominantly homosexual or merely a celebration of youthful beauty which happened to be male? Did their sequence matter much? Who were the several addressees – the young man who inspired most of those numbered up to 126 and the 'dark lady' who is the subject of most of the rest? Who was the mistress stolen from Shakespeare by a friend (40, also 41 and 42)? Theories have come and gone, some of them prospering, but no definitive answers are likely ever to be determined. The homosexual question is spectacularly unimportant since the great majority of sonnets 1–126 are not gender-specific. Their celebration of beauty and love is easily transferable between the sexes, which is why poems addressed almost certainly to a man have become world-famous as expressions of heterosexual love.

The form of these poems is of special interest. The sonnet, which had been imported from Italy, was proving difficult to handle in England since our language is not so rich in rhymes as Italian. Shakespeare settled on a new formula which involved using seven rhymes over the fourteen lines, rather than only four or five. His famous rhyme-scheme runs as follows: *abab cdcd efef gg*. This arrangement puts a great strain of responsibility on those last two lines, though Shakespeare proved adept at exploiting them in order to comment on the content of the first twelve lines, providing emphasis or, more commonly, subverting it or overturning it completely (as in 30 and 66).

Having rendered the form of the sonnet usable in a natural way, Shakespeare took care also to modernise its content. He made it clear that he was not addressing some ethereal creation, but a real person. Whereas Henry Constable had described his mistress walking in the garden as if she were a kind of rarefied spirit, Shakespeare wrote, amusingly and provocatively, 'My mistress, when she walks, treads on the ground' (130). This is not just a nice little joke. Shakespeare's sonnets have become canonised as some of the most beautiful and powerful expressions of love in the language for one good reason – they have every appearance of being rooted in intense personal experience rather than theory or fiction.

The sonnets cover many aspects of erotic experience. First, they celebrate youth and beauty (104) and even suggest that these fragile commodities might be preservable by art (18, 55). Love is seen as a unifying force (36), a transforming power that makes life worthwhile despite its discouragements (29, 30, 66), something transcendent (91) and inexpressible (106). When it is (apparently) not returned you suffer sadness and agony (145); when you are in love you are likely to be blinded to both reality (137, 141) and truth (138, 148). You will seem to be enslaved, and will not wish things otherwise (57, 149). Despite all the anguish and the problems of love, you will hope for its constancy and renewal (56, 116). When it works, life will seem too good to be true (49, 73).

As to sex, this is not treated with quite the frankness that you will get elsewhere in Shakespeare, though there are plenty of hints at the physical side of things. Sonnet 138, for example, deals ostensibly with truth and falsehood, but the entire piece was clearly constructed around its penultimate line which allows a rather ponderous *double entendre*: 'Therefore I lie with her and she with me'. Much more explicit is Sonnet 151, which rises and falls repeatedly in phallic virtuosity. Some few of the sonnets are, if judged by the highest standards, rather dull, repetitive or unsuccessfully experimental, but most of them strike home with some new vision of erotic experience. A dozen or so are true gems of English poetry, unforgettably sharp-edged and glittering with an individual beauty with which today's lovers will still wish to identify.

Songs from the Plays

Apart from the Histories and the Roman pieces, virtually all of Shakespeare's plays are decorated with songs. There are more than a hundred, authorship being sometimes dubious since the playwright may have used some existing material. *As You Like It* contains the most songs – no fewer than a dozen. These ornamentations vary in significance. Sometimes they are merely decorative; not infrequently, however, they carry a hidden poignancy which drives home one of the main ideas of the play with particular force. Much depends on context. In *Othello*, for instance, Desdemona sings a sad song of false love, 'The poor Soul sat sighing by a Sycamour Tree . . .', which cannot fail to move the audience because it has already had associations with death and clearly presages the death of this heroine. By contrast, in *Twelfth Night* a song about death itself, 'Come away, come away, Death . . .', is more whimsical than disturbing because it is merely a hyperbolical expression of love in the abstract, sung by a clown and with a surrounding context devoid of seriousness.

Most of the songs are about love in one form or another. Beauty is celebrated in both the much-loved song, 'Who is Silvia?' (*The Two Gentlemen of Verona*) and the hymn to Rosalind in *As You Like It*. Love is raised to an elevated plane of stylisation in 'If Love make me forsworn' and 'So sweet a Kiss . . .' (*Love's Labour's Lost*). It falls to a more prosaic level in 'Do nothing but eat' (*Henry IV, Part 2*), when we are told that 'Flesh is cheap and Females dear', in 'The Master, the Swabber' (*The Tempest*) and 'Was this fair Face . . . ?' (*All's Well That Ends Well*). Love's association with youthfulness is a common theme, often linked with the *carpe diem* message, as in 'It was a Lover, and his Lass . . .' (*As You Like It*). Sometimes love is seen as leading to pain and death ('Come away, come away, Death'), but you are just as likely to be reminded that this rhetorical concept is not part of real life; in *Troilus and Cressida* Pandarus tells us that the 'O ho' of a dying lover soon turns to 'ha ha ha'. Along with love comes marriage, and several songs, such as 'Wedding is great Juno's Crown' in *As You Like It*, celebrate this institution. But marriage often declines into infidelity and cuckoldry, which, if anything, is given greater prominence in Shakespeare's songs; a good example may be seen in 'Spring' (*Love's Labour's Lost*) which tells us that

> The cuckow then on ev'ry Tree
> Mocks Marri'd Men: for thus sings he,
>   'Cuckow.'
> 'Cuckow, cuckow': O Word of Fear,
> Unpleasing to a Marri'd Ear.

The love-songs are by and large not overtly sexual. Ophelia's well-known and rather surprising hints at sexuality in 'To morrow is Saint Valentine's Day' are the exception rather than the rule. Occasionally, however, Shakespeare's famous taste for bawdy has to do with the singing of songs. Perhaps the best example is in *Cymbeline*, when musicians are summoned by Cloten to sing a morning serenade to Imogen. The surrounding conversation, which has much to do with penetration, fingering and trying with the tongue, leaves little for the imagination to invent for itself.

The Plays

Similar topics are pursued in many of the plays, to which any aspiring English-speaking lover should turn for amorous quotation. Here the sentiments prettily presented in the sonnets and delicately hinted at in song may be seen and heard fully expounded. If you want beauty and splendour turn immediately to the description of Cleopatra in her barge or perhaps the opening of Act V of *The Merchant of Venice* ('The Moon shines bright. In such a Night as this'). Love in its sublimest character is celebrated in *Romeo and Juliet*, when the hero begins the most famous love-scene in world literature with the words

> But soft, what Light through yonder Window breaks?
> It is the East, and Juliet is the Sun.

and soon after she responds with the famous soliloquy beginning, 'Gallop apace, you fiery footed Steeds', which contains the heart-melting plea (at once a continuation of his stellar metaphor and a presentiment of their double death)

> Give me my Romeo, and when I shall die,
> Take him and cut him out in little Stars,
> And he will make the Face of Heaven so fine
> That all the World will be in love with Night
> And pay no Worship to the garish Sun.

Greater eloquence in the telling of love would be hard to discover within the limitations of language. On the other hand, Shakespeare's plays show no less interest in love at lower levels. If you want down-to-earth directness on the subject consult Parolles's amusing discourse on virginity ('away with 't.') in *All's Well That Ends Well*. A delicious depiction of healthy female love spilling over into lust may be seen in Cleopatra's thoughts about Antony: 'O happy Horse, to bear the weight of Antony!' Love at its silliest is portrayed by Armado early in *Love's Labour's Lost*, who ends up babbling, 'Adieu, Valour! Rust, Rapier! Be still, Drum! For your Manager is in Love; yea, he loveth. Assist me some extemporal God of Rime, for I am sure I shall turn Sonneter. Devise, Wit! Write, Pen! For I am for whole Volumes in Folio.' Can this be the same language as used by Juliet?

In the first act of *A Midsummer Night's Dream* Lysander makes an epigrammatic comment which has become famous: 'The Course of True Love never did run smooth.' The lack of smoothness is explored by the master in some detail, with all its tragic and comic consequences, bringing out different reactions. In *Twelfth Night*

Viola, disguised as a man, describes herself obliquely as being 'like Patience on a Monument', waiting for her love to become fulfilled. The opposite attitude is shown by the formidable Kate in *The Taming of the Shrew*, informed by Petruchio that their wedding day is on Sunday she tells him, 'I'll see thee hang'd on Sunday first!'

No one can control the forces of love, which are variously depicted as blind, fantastical, utterly overwhelming. It has a twofold association with death, to which it consigns Shakespeare's tragic heroines and towards which it steers many a comic hero. Lord Berowne (*Love's Labour's Lost*) puts the point succinctly: 'By the Lord, this Love is as Mad as Aiax: it kills Sheep, it kills me, I a Sheep.' Valentine, one of the two gentlemen of Verona, considers death as an alternative to living without Silvia's love: 'And why not Death rather than living Torment?' But for every repining hero of this ilk there are two or three with a more pragmatic attitude to love. Henry V, no gallant of the honeyed word, woos his Kate with endearing frankness. 'I speak to thee plain Soldier. If thou canst love me for this, take me. If not, to say to thee that I shall die is true; but for thy Love, by the Lord, no.' Rosalind in *As You Like It* matches these sentiments when confronted with Orlando, an aspiring lover who talks of death: 'the poor World is almost six thousand years old, and in all this Time there was not any Man died in his own Person, *videlicet*, in a Love Cause.' The entire business of dying for love is wonderfully parodied in the tragedy of Pyramus and Thisby in the last act of *A Midsummer Night's Dream*.

Shakespeare's grasp of the subject of love is comprehensive, and deeply grounded in experience. His personal entanglement with Eros must have begun early – by the age of eighteen he married a woman eight years older who was three months pregnant – and seems to have been extensive and long-lasting. It is our good fortune that he survived long enough in a dangerous age to speak out across the entire range of this mysterious and powerful force. The fullest expression of Love, with all its energy and wonder, requires the finest powers of language. For this we need poetry, and we need Shakespeare, the greatest of our love poets.

A.D.P. BRIGGS

The Sonnets

18

Shall I compare thee to a summer's day?
Thou art more lovely and more temperate:
Rough winds do shake the darling buds of May,
And summer's lease hath all too short a date:
Sometime too hot the eye of heaven shines,
And often is his gold complexion dimm'd;
And every fair from fair sometime declines,
By chance or nature's changing course untrimm'd;
But thy eternal summer shall not fade,
Nor lose possession of that fair thou owest;
Nor shall Death brag thou wander'st in his shade,
When in eternal lines to time thou grow'st:
    So long as men can breathe, or eyes can see,
    So long lives this, and this gives life to thee.

29

When, in disgrace with fortune and men's eyes,
I all alone beweep my outcast state,
And trouble deaf heaven with my bootless cries,
And look upon myself, and curse my fate,
Wishing me like to one more rich in hope,
Featured like him, like him with friends possess'd,
Desiring this man's art and that man's scope,
With what I most enjoy contented least;
Yet in these thoughts myself almost despising,
Haply I think on thee, and then my state,
Like to the lark at break of day arising
From sullen earth, sings hymns at heaven's gate;
    For thy sweet love remember'd such wealth brings
    That then I scorn to change my state with kings.

30

When to the sessions of sweet silent thought
I summon up remembrance of things past,
I sigh the lack of many a thing I sought,
And with old woes new wail my dear time's waste:
Then can I drown an eye, unused to flow,
For precious friends hid in death's dateless night,
And weep afresh love's long since cancell'd woe,
And moan the expense of many a vanish'd sight:
Then can I grieve at grievances foregone,
And heavily from woe to woe tell o'er
The sad account of fore-bemoaned moan,
Which I new pay as if not paid before.
    But if the while I think on thee, dear friend,
    All losses are restored and sorrows end.

36

Let me confess that we two must be twain,
Although our undivided loves are one:
So shall those blots that do with me remain,
Without thy help, by me be borne alone.
In our two loves there is but one respect,
Though in our lives a separable spite,
Which though it alter not love's sole effect,
Yet doth it steal sweet hours from love's delight.
I may not evermore acknowledge thee,
Lest my bewailed guilt should do thee shame,
Nor thou with public kindness honour me,
Unless thou take that honour from thy name:
  But do not so; I love thee in such sort,
  As thou being mine, mine is thy good report.

40

Take all my loves, my love, yea, take them all;
What hast thou then more than thou hadst before?
No love, my love, that thou mayst true love call;
All mine was thine before thou hadst this more.
Then, if for my love thou my love receivest,
I cannot blame thee for my love thou usest;
But yet be blamed, if thou thyself deceivest
By wilful taste of what thyself refusest.
I do forgive thy robbery, gentle thief,
Although thou steal thee all my poverty;
And yet, love knows, it is a greater grief
To bear love's wrong than hate's known injury.
    Lascivious grace, in whom all ill well shows,
    Kill me with spites; yet we must not be foes.

49

Against that time, if ever that time come,
When I shall see thee frown on my defects,
When as thy love hath cast his utmost sum,
Call'd to that audit by advised respects;
Against that time when thou shalt strangely pass,
And scarcely greet me with that sun, thine eye,
When love, converted from the thing it was,
Shall reasons find of settled gravity;
Against that time do I ensconce me here
Within the knowledge of mine own desert,
And this my hand against myself uprear,
To guard the lawful reasons on thy part:
  To leave poor me thou hast the strength of laws,
  Since why to love I can allege no cause.

51

Thus can my love excuse the slow offence
Of my dull bearer when from thee I speed:
From where thou art why should I haste me thence?
Till I return, of posting is no need.
O, what excuse will my poor beast then find,
When swift extremity can seem but slow?
Then should I spur, though mounted on the wind,
In winged speed no motion shall I know:
Then can no horse with my desire keep pace;
Therefore desire, of perfect'st love being made,
Shall neigh–no dull flesh–in his fiery race;
But love, for love, thus shall excuse my jade;
    Since from thee going he went wilful-slow,
    Towards thee I'll run and give him leave to go.

55

Not marble, nor the gilded monuments
Of princes, shall outlive this powerful rhyme?
But you shall shine more bright in these contents
Than unswept stone besmear'd with sluttish time.
When wasteful war shall statues overturn,
And broils root out the work of masonry,
Nor Mars his sword nor war's quick fire shall burn
The living record of your memory.
'Gainst death and all-oblivious enmity
Shall you pace forth; your praise shall still find room
Even in the eyes of all posterity
That wear this world out to the ending doom.
    So, till the judgement that yourself arise,
    You live in this, and dwell in lovers' eyes.

56

Sweet love, renew thy force; be it not said
Thy edge should blunter be than appetite,
Which but to-day by feeding is allay'd,
To-morrow sharpen'd in his former might:
So, love, be thou; although to-day thou fill
Thy hungry eyes even till they wink with fulness,
To-morrow see again, and do not kill
The spirit of love with a perpetual dulness.
Let this sad interim like the ocean be
Which parts the shore, where two contracted new
Come daily to the banks, that, when they see
Return of love, more blest may be the view;
    Or call it winter, which, being full of care,
    Makes summer's welcome thrice more wish'd, more rare.

57

Being your slave, what should I do but tend
Upon the hours and times of your desire?
I have no precious time at all to spend,
Nor services to do, till you require.
Nor dare I chide the world-without-end hour
Whilst I, my sovereign, watch the clock for you,
Nor think the bitterness of absence sour
When you have bid your servant once adieu;
Nor dare I question with my jealous thought
Where you may be, or your affairs suppose,
But, like a sad slave, stay and think of nought
Save, where you are how happy you make those.
    So true a fool is love that in your will,
    Though you do any thing, he thinks no ill.

66

Tired with all these, for restful death I cry,
As, to behold desert a beggar born,
And needy nothing trimm'd in jollity,
And purest faith unhappily forsworn,
And gilded honour shamefully misplaced,
And maiden virtue rudely strumpeted,
And right perfection wrongfully disgraced,
And strength by limping sway disabled,
And art made tongue-tied by authority,
And folly, doctor-like, controlling skill,
And simple truth miscall'd simplicity,
And captive good attending captain ill:
    Tired with all these, from these would I be gone,
    Save that, to die, I leave my love alone.

71

No longer mourn for me when I am dead
Than you shall hear the surly sullen bell
Give warning to the world that I am fled
From this vile world, with vilest worms to dwell:
Nay, if you read this line, remember not
The hand that writ it; for I love you so,
That I in your sweet thoughts would be forgot,
If thinking on me then should make you woe.
O, if, I say, you look upon this verse
When I perhaps compounded am with clay,
Do not so much as my poor name rehearse,
But let your love even with my life decay;
    Lest the wise world should look into your moan,
    And mock you with me after I am gone.

73

That time of year thou mayst in me behold
When yellow leaves, or none, or few, do hang
Upon those boughs which shake against the cold,
Bare ruin'd choirs, where late the sweet birds sang.
In me thou see'st the twilight of such day
As after sunset fadeth in the west;
Which by and by black night doth take away,
Death's second self, that seals up all in rest.
In me thou see'st the glowing of such fire,
That on the ashes of his youth doth lie,
As the death-bed whereon it must expire,
Consumed with that which it was nourish'd by.
    This thou perceiv'st, which makes thy love more strong,
    To love that well which thou must leave ere long.

91

Some glory in their birth, some in their skill,
Some in their wealth, some in their body's force;
Some in their garments, though new-fangled ill;
Some in their hawks and hounds, some in their horse;
And every humour hath his adjunct pleasure,
Wherein it finds a joy above the rest:
But these particulars are not my measure;
All these I better in one general best.
Thy love is better than high birth to me,
Richer than wealth, prouder than garments' cost,
Of more delight than hawks or horses be;
And having thee, of all men's pride I boast:
	Wretched in this alone, that thou mayst take
	All this away and me most wretched make.

97

How like a winter hath my absence been
From thee, the pleasure of the fleeting year!
What freezings have I felt, what dark days seen!
What old December's bareness every where!
And yet this time removed was summer's time;
The teeming autumn, big with rich increase,
Bearing the wanton burthen of the prime,
Like widowed wombs after their lords' decease:
Yet this abundant issue seem'd to me
But hope of orphans and unfather'd fruit;
For summer and his pleasures wait on thee,
And, thou away, the very birds are mute;
  Or, if they sing, 'tis with so dull a cheer
  That leaves look pale, dreading the winter's near.

102

My love is strengthen'd, though more weak in seeming;
I love not less, though less the show appear:
That love is merchandized whose rich esteeming
The owner's tongue doth publish every where.
Our love was new, and then but in the spring,
When I was wont to greet it with my lays;
As Philomel in summer's front doth sing,
And stops her pipe in growth of riper days:
Not that the summer is less pleasant now
Than when her mournful hymns did hush the night
But that wild music burthens every bough,
And sweets grown common lose their dear delight.
    Therefore, like her, I sometime hold my tongue,
    Because I would not dull you with my song.

104

To me, fair friend, you never can be old,
For as you were when first your eye I eyed,
Such seems your beauty still. Three winters cold
Have from the forests shook three summers' pride,
Three beauteous springs to yellow autumn turn'd
In process of the seasons have I seen,
Three April perfumes in three hot Junes burn'd,
Since first I saw you fresh, which yet are green.
Ah, yet doth beauty, like a dial-hand,
Steal from his figure, and no pace perceived;
So your sweet hue, which methinks still doth stand,
Hath motion, and mine eye may be deceived:
 For fear of which, hear this, thou age unbred;
 Ere you were born was beauty's summer dead.

105

Let not my love be call'd idolatry,
Nor my beloved as an idol show,
Since all alike my songs and praises be
To one, of one, still such, and ever so.
Kind is my love to-day, to-morrow kind
Still constant in a wondrous excellence;
Therefore my verse to constancy confined,
One thing expressing, leaves out difference.
'Fair, kind, and true,' is all my argument,
'Fair, kind, and true,' varying to other words;
And in this change is my invention spent,
Three themes in one, which wondrous scope affords.
    'Fair, kind, and true,' have often lived alone,
    Which three till now never kept seat in one.

106

When in the chronicle of wasted time
I see descriptions of the fairest wights,
And beauty making beautiful old rhyme
In praise of ladies dead and lovely knights,
Then, in the blazon of sweet beauty's best,
Of hand, of foot, of lip, of eye, of brow,
I see their antique pen would have express'd
Even such a beauty as you master now.
So all their praises are but prophecies
Of this our time, all you prefiguring;
And, for they look'd but with divining eyes,
They had not skill enough your worth to sing:
    For we, which now behold these present days,
    Have eyes to wonder, but lack tongues to praise.

116

Let me not to the marriage of true minds
Admit impediments. Love is not love
Which alters when it alteration finds,
Or bends with the remover to remove:
O, no! it is an ever-fixed mark,
That looks on tempests and is never shaken;
It is the star to every wandering bark,
Whose worth's unknown, although his height be taken.
Love's not Time's fool, though rosy lips and cheeks
Within his bending sickle's compass come;
Love alters not with his brief hours and weeks,
But bears it out even to the edge of doom.
    If this be error and upon me proved,
    I never writ, nor no man ever loved.

130

My mistress' eyes are nothing like the sun;
Coral is far more red than her lips' red:
If snow be white, why then her breasts are dun;
If hairs be wires, black wires grow on her head.
I have seen roses damask'd, red and white,
But no such roses see I in her cheeks;
And in some perfumes is there more delight
Than in the breath that from my mistress reeks.
I love to hear her speak, yet well I know
That music hath a far more pleasing sound:
I grant I never saw a goddess go,
My mistress, when she walks, treads on the ground:
    And yet, by heaven, I think my love as rare
    As any she belied with false compare.

137

Thou blind fool, Love, what dost thou to mine eyes,
That they behold, and see not what they see?
They know what beauty is, see where it lies,
Yet what the best is take the worst to be.
If eyes, corrupt by over-partial looks,
Be anchor'd in the bay where all men ride,
Why of eyes' falsehood hast thou forged hooks,
Whereto the judgement of my heart is tied?
Why should my heart think that a several plot
Which my heart knows the wide world's common place?
Or mine eyes seeing this, say this is not,
To put fair truth upon so foul a face?
    In things right true my heart and eyes have erred,
    And to this false plague are they now transferred.

138

When my love swears that she is made of truth,
I do believe her, though I know she lies,
That she might think me some untutor'd youth,
Unlearned in the world's false subtleties.
Thus vainly thinking that she thinks me young,
Although she knows my days are past the best,
Simply I credit her false-speaking tongue:
On both sides thus is simple truth suppress'd.
But wherefore says she not she is unjust?
And wherefore say not I that I am old?
O, love's best habit is in seeming trust,
And age in love loves not to have years told:
    Therefore I lie with her and she with me,
    And in our faults by lies we flatter'd be.

141

In faith, I do not love thee with mine eyes,
For they in thee a thousand errors note;
But 'tis my heart that loves what they despise,
Who, in despite of view, is pleased to dote;
Nor are mine ears with thy tongue's tune delighted;
Nor tender feeling, to base touches prone,
Nor taste, nor smell, desire to be invited
To any sensual feast with thee alone:
But my five wits nor my five senses can
Dissuade one foolish heart from serving thee,
Who leaves unsway'd the likeness of a man,
Thy proud heart's slave and vassal wretch to be:
　　　Only my plague thus far I count my gain,
　　　That she that makes me sin awards me pain.

142

Love is my sin, and thy dear virtue hate,
Hate of my sin, grounded on sinful loving:
O, but with mine compare thou thine own state,
And thou shalt find it merits not reproving;
Or, if it do, not from those lips of thine,
That have profaned their scarlet ornaments
And seal'd false bonds of love as oft as mine,
Robb'd others' beds' revenues of their rents.
Be it lawful I love thee, as thou lovest those
Whom thine eyes woo as mine importune thee:
Root pity in thy heart, that, when it grows,
Thy pity may deserve to pitied be.
     If thou dost seek to have what thou dost hide,
     By self-example mayst thou be denied!

145

Those lips that Love's own hand did make
Breathed forth the sound that said 'I hate,'
To me that languish'd for her sake:
But when she saw my woeful state,
Straight in her heart did mercy come,
Chiding that tongue that ever sweet
Was used in giving gentle doom;
And taught it thus anew to greet;
'I hate' she alter'd with an end,
That follow'd it as gentle day
Doth follow night, who, like a fiend,
From heaven to hell is flown away;
    'I hate' from hate away she threw,
    And saved my life, saying 'not you.'

147

My love is as a fever, longing still
For that which longer nurseth the disease;
Feeding on that which doth preserve the ill,
The uncertain sickly appetite to please.
My reason, the physician to my love,
Angry that his prescriptions are not kept,
Hath left me, and I desperate now approve,
Desire is death, which physic did except.
Past cure I am, now reason is past care,
And frantic-mad with evermore unrest;
My thoughts and my discourse as madmen's are,
At random from the truth vainly express'd;
  For I have sworn thee fair, and thought thee bright,
  Who art as black as hell, as dark as night.

148

O, me, what eyes hath Love put in my head,
Which have no correspondence with true sight!
Or, if they have, where is my judgement fled,
That censures falsely what they see aright?
If that be fair whereon my false eyes dote,
What means the world to say it is not so?
If it be not, then love doth well denote
Love's eye is not so true as all men's: no,
How can it? O, how can Love's eye be true,
That is so vex'd with watching and with tears?
No marvel then, though I mistake my view;
The sun itself sees not till heaven clears.
    O cunning Love! with tears thou keep'st me blind,
    Lest eyes well-seeing thy foul faults should find.

149

Canst thou, O cruel! say I love thee not,
When I against myself with thee partake?
Do I not think on thee, when I forgot
Am of myself, all tyrant, for thy sake?
Who hateth thee that I do call my friend?
On whom frown'st thou that I do fawn upon?
Nay, if thou lour'st on me, do I not spend
Revenge upon myself with present moan?
What merit do I in myself respect,
That is so proud thy service to despise,
When all my best doth worship thy defect,
Commanded by the motion of thine eyes?
    But, love, hate on, for now I know thy mind;
    Those that can see thou lovest, and I am blind.

151

Love is too young to know what conscience is;
Yet who knows not conscience is born of love?
Then, gentle cheater, urge not my amiss,
Lest guilty of my faults thy sweet self prove:
For, thou betraying me, I do betray
My nobler part to my gross body's treason;
My soul doth tell my body that he may
Triumph in love; flesh stays no farther reason,
But rising at thy name doth point out thee
As his triumphant prize. Proud of this pride,
He is contented thy poor drudge to be,
To stand in thy affairs, fall by thy side.
    No want of conscience hold it that I call
    Her 'love' for whose dear love I rise and fall.

Songs from the Plays

For I the Ballad will repeat,
  Which men full true shall find:
Your Marriage comes by Destiny,
  Your Cuckow sings by Kind.

All's Well That Ends Well (I, iii)

'Was this fair Face the Cause,' quoth she,
   'Why the Grecians sacked Troy?
Fond done, done fond,
   Was this King Priam's Joy?'
With that she sighed as she stood,
With that she sighed as she stood,
   And gave this Sentence then:
'Among Nine Bad if One be Good,
Among Nine Bad if One be Good,
   There's yet One Good in Ten.'

All's Well That Ends Well (I, iii)

From the East to Western Inde,
    no Jewel is like Rosalinde,
Her Worth, being mounted on the Wind,
    through all the World bears Rosalinde.
All the Pictures fairest lin'd
    are but black to Rosalinde;
Let no face be kept in mind
    but the fair of Rosalinde.
If a Hart do lack a Hind,
    let him seek out Rosalinde;
If the Cat will after kind,
    so be sure will Rosalinde.
Wint'red Garments must be lin'd,
    so must slender Rosalinde:
They that reap must sheaf and bind,
    then to Cart with Rosalinde.
Sweetest Nut hath sowrest Rind,
    such a Nut is Rosalinde.
He that sweetest Rose will find
    must find Love's Prick, and Rosalinde.

As You Like It (III, ii)

Art thou God, to Shepherd turn'd?
That a Maiden's Heart hath burn'd.
Why, thy Godhead laid a part,
Warr'st thou with a Woman's Heart?
Whiles the Eye of Man did woo me,
That could do no Vengeance to me.
If the Scorn of your bright Eyne
Have Power to raise such Love in mine,
Alack, in me what strange Effect
Would they work in mild Aspect?
Whiles you chid me, I did love,
How then might your Prayers move?
He that brings this Love to thee
Little knows this Love in me:
And by him seal up thy Mind,
Whether that thy Youth and Kind
Will the faithful Offer take
Of me, and all that I can make,
Or else by him my Love deny,
And then I'll study how to die.

As You Like It (IV, iii)

It was a Lover, and his Lass,
  With a hey, and a ho, and a hey nonino,
That o'er the green corn Field did pass,
  In Spring Time, the onely pretty Ring Time.
When Birds do sing, hey ding a ding, ding:
Sweet Lovers love the Spring.

Between the Acres of the Rye,
  With a hey, and a ho, and a hey nonino,
These pretty Country-folks would lie,
  In Spring Time, the onely pretty Ring Time.
When Birds do sing, hey ding a ding, ding:
Sweet Lovers love the Spring.

This Carol they began that Hour,
  With a hey, and a ho, and a hey nonino:
How that a Life was but a Flower,
  In Spring Time, the onely pretty Ring Time.
When Birds do sing, hey ding a ding, ding:
Sweet Lovers love the Spring.

And therefore take the present Time,
  With a hey, and a ho, and a hey nonino,
For Love is crowned with the Prime,
  In Spring Time, the onely pretty Ring Time.
When Birds do sing, hey ding a ding, ding:
Sweet Lovers love the Spring.

As You Like It (V, iii)

Wedding is great Juno's Crown,
　O blessed Bond of Boord and Bed;
'Tis Hymen peoples every Town,
　High Wedlock then be honoured;
Honour, high Honour and Renown
To Hymen, God of every Town.

As You Like It (V, iv)

Fear no more the Heat o'th' Sun,
　　Nor the furious Winter's Rages,
Thou thy worldly Task hast done,
　　Home art gone, and ta'en thy Wages.
　　　　Golden Lads and Girls all must,
　　　　　As Chimney-Sweepers, come to Dust.

Fear no more the Frown o'th' Great,
　　Thou art past the Tyrant's Stroke;
Care no more to clothe and eat,
　　To thee the Reed is as the Oak.
　　　　The Scepter, Learning, Physic, must
　　　　　All follow this and come to Dust.

Fear no more the Lightning-flash.
　　Nor th' all-dreaded Thunderstone.
Fear not Slander, Censure rash.
　　Thou hast finish'd Joy and Moan.
　　　　All Lovers young, all Lovers must
　　　　　Consign to thee and come to Dust.

No Exorcisor harm thee.
　　Nor no Witchcraft charm thee.
Ghost unlaid forbear thee.
　　Nothing ill come near thee.
　　　　Quiet Consummation have,
　　　　　And renowned be thy Grave.

Cymbeline (IV, ii)

' "How should I your True-love know
    From another one?"
"By his Cockle Hat and Staff,
    And his Sandal Shoone." '

' "He is dead and gone, Lady,
    He is dead and gone:
At his Head a Grass-green Turf,
    At his Heels a Stone." '

'White his Shrowd as the Mountain Snow.'
    'Larded all with sweet Flowers,
Which, beweept to the Ground, did not go
    With True-love Showers.'

                    Hamlet (IV, v)

'To morrow is Saint Valentine's Day,
    All in the Morning betime,
And I a Maid at your Window
    To be your Valentine.

    Then up he rose,
    And donn'd his Clothes,
And dupp'd the Chamber Door;
    Let in the Maid
    That out a Maid
Never departed more.'

'By Gis and by Saint Charity,
    Alack and fie for Shame,
Young Men will do't if they come to't,
    By Cock they are too blame.'

Quoth she, ' "Before you tumbled me,
    You promis'd me to wed." '
' "So would I 'a done, by Yonder Sun,
    And Thou hadst not come to my Bed." '

Hamlet (IV, v)

'In Youth when I did love, did love,
  Me thought it was very sweet
To contract, O, the Time for a my Behove,
  O me thought there a was nothing a meet.'

'But Age with his stealing Steps
  Hath claw'd me in his Clutch,
And hath shipp'd me intill the Land
  As if I had never been such.'

'A Pickaxe and a Spade, a Spade,
  For and a Shrowding Sheet.
O a Pit of Clay for to be made
  For such a Guest is meet.'

Hamlet (V, i)

Do nothing but eat and make good Cheer,
And praise God for the merry Year,
When Flesh is cheap and Females dear,
And lusty Lads roam here and there
        So merrily,
And ever among so merrily.

Be merry, be merry. My Wife has all,
For Women are Shrows, both short and tall;
'Tis merry in Hall when Beards wags all,
        And welcome Merry Shrovetide;
Be merry, be merry.

Henry IV, Part 2 (V, iii)

If Love make me forsworn, how shall I swear to love?
Ah never Faith could hold, if not to Beauty vowed.
Though to my self forsworn, to thee I'll faithful prove.
Those Thoughts to me were Oaks, to thee like Osiers bowed.
Study his Bias leaves, and makes his Book thine Eyes,
Where all those Pleasures live that Art would comprehend.
If Knowledge be the Mark, to know thee shall suffice.
Well Learned is that Tongue that well can thee commend,
All Ignorant that Soul that sees thee without Wonder.
Which is to me some Praise, that I thy Parts admire.
Thy Eye Jove's Lightning bears, thy Voice his dreadful Thunder,
Which, not to Anger bent, is Music and sweet Fire.
Celestial as thou art, O pardon, Love, this Wrong,
That singes Heaven's Praise with such an Earthly Tongue.

Love's Labour's Lost (IV, ii)

So sweet a Kiss the golden Sun gives not
To those fresh Morning Drops upon the Rose
As thy Eye beams when their fresh Rays have smot
The Night of Dew that on my Cheeks down flows;
Nor shines the silver Moon one half so bright
Through the transparent Bosom of the Deep
As doth thy Face through Tears of mine give Light.
Thou shin'st in ev'ry Tear that I do weep:
No Drop but as a Coach doth carry thee,
So ridest thou triumphing in my Woe.
Do but behold the Tears that swell in me,
And they thy Glory through my Grief will show.
But do not love thy self: then thou wilt keep
My Tears for Glasses, and still make me weep.
O Queen of Queens, how far doost thou excel
No Thought can think, nor Tongue of Mortal tell.

Love's Labour's Lost (IV, iii)

When Daisies pied, and Violets blew,
And Cuckow-buds of Yellow Hew,
And Lady-smocks all Silver-white,
Do paint the Meadows with Delight,
The Cuckow then on ev'ry Tree
Mocks Marri'd Men: for thus sings he,
   'Cuckow.'
'Cuckow, Cuckow': O Word of Fear,
Unpleasing to a Marri'd Ear.

When Shepherds pipe on Oaten Straws,
And merry Larks are Ploughmen's Clocks,
When Turtles tread, and Rooks and Daws,
And Maidens bleach their Summer Smocks,
The Cuckow then on ev'ry Tree
Mocks Marri'd Men, for thus sings he,
   'Cuckow.'
'Cuckow, Cuckow': O Word of Fear,
Unpleasing to a Marri'd Ear.

Love's Labour's Lost (V. ii)

Take, oh take those Lips away
   That so sweetly were forsworn,
And those Eyes, the break of Day,
   Lights that do mislead the Morn;
     But my Kisses bring again, bring again,
     Seals of Love, but seal'd in vain, seal'd in vain.

Measure for Measure (IV, i)

Fie on sinful Fantasy,
Fie on Lust and Luxury!
Lust is but a bloody Fire,
Kindled with unchaste Desire,
Fed in Heart whose Flames aspire
As Thoughts do blow them higher and higher.
Pinch him, Fairies, mutually,
Pinch him for his Villainy!
Pinch him, and burn him, and turn him about,
Till Candles, and Starlight, and Moonshine be out.

The Merry Wives of Windsor (V, v)

Sigh no more Ladies, sigh no more:
    Men were Deceivers ever,
One Foot in Sea, and one on Shore,
    To one thing constant never,
Then sigh not so, but let them go,
    And be you blithe and bonny,
Converting all your Sounds of Woe
    Into hey nonny nonny.

Sing no more Ditties, sing no moe
    Of Dumps so dull and heavy;
The Fraud of Men was ever so
    Since Summer first was leavy.
Then sigh not so, but let them go,
    And be you blithe and bonny,
Converting all your Sounds of Woe
    Into hey nonny nonny.

Much Ado About Nothing (II, iii)

The poor Soul sat sighing by
        a Sycamour Tree,
Sing all a green Willow;
    Her Hand on her Bosom,
        her Head on her Knee,
Sing Willow, Willow, Willow.

    The fresh Streams ran by her,
        and murmur'd her Moans:
Sing Willow, Willow, Willow.
    Her salt Tears fell from her,
        and soft'ned the Stones:
Sing Willow, Willow, Willow.

Sing all a green Willow
        must be my Garland.
    Let no body blame him,
        his Scorn I approve.

I call'd my Love False Love:
        but what said he then?
Sing Willow, Willow, Willow.
    If I court moe Women,
        you'll couch with moe Men.

Othello (IV, iii)

The Master, the Swabber, the Boatswain, and I,
    The Gunner, and his Mate,
Lov'd Mall, Meg, and Marian, and Margerie,
    But none of us car'd for Kate.
    For she had a Tongue with a Tang,
    Would cry to a Sailor 'Go hang.'
She lov'd not the Savour of Tar nor of Pitch,
Yet a Tailor might scratch her where e'er she did itch.
    Then to Sea, Boys, and let her go hang.

The Tempest (II, ii)

Honour, Riches, Marriage, Blessing,
Long continuance, and increasing;
Hourly Joys be still upon you,
Juno sings her Blessings on you.
Earth's Increase, Foison plenty;
Barns and Garners never empty.
Vines, with clust'ring Bunches growing,
Plants, with goodly Burthen bowing;
Spring come to you at the farthest
In the very end of Harvest.
Scarcity and Want shall shun you,
Ceres' Blessing so is on you.

The Tempest (IV, i)

Love, Love, nothing but Love,
 Still love still more;
  For O Love's Bow
  Shoots Buck and Doe;
   The Shaft confounds
   Not that it wounds,
 But tickles still the Sore.
  These Lovers cry,
  O ho, they die,
Yet that which seems the Wound to kill
 Doth turn 'O ho' to 'Ha ha he';
So dying Love lives still,
 'O ho' a while, but ha ha ha,
 'O ho' groans out for 'ha ha ha' –
  Hey ho.

Troilus and Cressida (III, i)

O Mistress mine, where are you roaming?
O stay and hear: your true Love's coming,
   That can sing both high and low.
Trip no further, pretty Sweeting:
Journeys end in Lovers Meeting,
   Every Wise Man's Son doth know.

What is Love, 'tis not hereafter,
Present Mirth hath present Laughter;
   What's to come is still unsure.
In Delay there lies no Plenty,
Then come kiss me sweet and twenty:
   Youth's a stuff will not endure.

Twelfth Night (II, iii)

Come away, come away, Death,
    And in sad Cypress let me be laid.
Fie away, fie away, Breath,
    I am slain by a fair cruel Maid.
My Shroud of White, stuck all with Yew,
        O prepare it.
My part of Death no one so true
        Did share it.

Not a Flower, not a Flower sweet
        On my black Coffin, let there be strewn;
Not a Friend, not a Friend greet
My poor Corpse, where my Bones shall be thrown.
A thousand thousand Sighs to save,
        Lay me O where
Sad true Lover never find my Grave,
        To weep there.

Twelfth Night (II, iv)

Who is Silvia? What is she?
That all our Swains commend her?
Holy, fair, and wise is she;
The Heaven such Grace did lend her
    That she might admired be.

Is she kind as she is fair?
For Beauty lives with Kindness.
Love doth to her Eyes repair
To help him of his Blindness,
    And, being helped, inhabits there.

Then to Silvia let us sing
That Silvia is excelling;
She excels each Mortal Thing
Upon the dull Earth dwelling.
    To her let us Garlands bring.

The Two Gentlemen of Verona (IV, ii)

Get you hence, for I must go
Where it fits not you to know.
   Whether?
              O whether?
                       Whether?
It becomes thy Oath full well,
Thou to me thy Secrets tell.
   Me too: let me go thether.
Or thou goest to th' Grange, or Mill;
If to either, thou dost ill.
   Neither.
           What, neither?
                    Neither.
Thou hast sworn my Love to be.
Thou hast sworn it more to me.
   Then whether goest? Say whether?

The Winter's Tale (IV, iv)

The Plays

HELENA I am undone: there is no Living, none,
    If Bertram be away. 'Twere all one
    That I should love a bright partic'lar Star
    And think to wed it, he is so above me;
    In his bright Radiance and collat'ral Light
    Must I be comforted, not in his Sphere.
    Th' Ambition in my Love thus plagues it self:
    The Hind that would be mated by the Lion
    Must die for Love. 'Twas pretty, though a Plague,
    To see him ev'ry Hour to sit and draw
    His arched Brows, his hawking Eye, his Curls,
    In our Heart's Table: Heart too capable
    Of ev'ry Line and Trick of his sweet Favor.
    But now he's gone, and my idolatrous Fancy
    Must sanctify his Reliques.

All's Well That Ends Well (I, i)

HELENA Bless our poor Virginity from
     Underminers and Blowers-up. Is there no
     Military Policy how Virgins might blow up Men?
PAROLLES Virginity being blown down, Man will
     quicklier be blown up; marry in blowing him
     down again, with the Breach your selves made,
     you lose your City. It is not Politic in the
     Commonwealth of Nature to preserve Virginity.
     Loss of Virginity is rational Increase; and there
     was never Virgin got till Virginity was first lost.
     That you were made of is Metal to make Virgins.
     Virginity, by being once Lost, may be ten times
     Found; by being ever Kept, it is ever Lost. 'Tis
     too cold a Companion: away with 't.

          All's Well That Ends Well (I, i)

CLEOPATRA   – O Charmian,
   Where think'st thou he is now? Stands he, or sits he?
   Or does he walk? Or is he on his Horse?
   Oh happy Horse, to bear the weight of Antony!
   Do bravely, Horse, for wot'st thou whom thou mov'st?
   The demi-Atlas of this Earth, the Arm
   And Burgonet of Men. He's speaking now,
   Or murmuring, 'Where's my Serpent of old Nile?'
   (For so he calls me). Now I feed my self
   With most delicious Poison.

                    Antony and Cleopatra (I, v)

ENOBARBUS   The Barge she sat in, like a burnish'd Throne,
     Burnt on the Water. The Poop was beaten Gold,
     Purple the Sails, and so perfumed that
     The Winds were Love-sick. With them the Owers were Silver,
     Which to the tune of Flutes kept stroke, and made
     The Water which they beat to follow faster,
     As amorous of their Strokes. For her own Person,
     It beggar'd all Description. She did lie
     In her Pavilion, Cloth of Gold of Tissue,
     O'er-picturing that Venus where we see
     The Fancy out-work Nature. On each side her
     Stood pretty dimpled Boys, like smiling Cupids,
     With divers colour'd Fans whose Wind did seem
     To glove the delicate Cheeks which they did cool,
     And what they undid did.

               Antony and Cleopatra (II, ii)

ROSALIND No faith, die by Attorney: the poor
World is almost six thousand years old, and in
all this Time there was not any Man died in his
own Person, *videlicet*, in a Love Cause. Troilus
had his Brains dash'd out with a Grecian Club,
yet he did what he could to die before, and he is
one of the Patterns of Love. Leander, he would
have liv'd many a fair year though Hero had
turn'd Nun, if it had not been for a hot
Midsummer-night; for, good Youth, he went but
forth to wash him in the Hellespont, and being
taken with the Cramp, was drown'd, and the
foolish Chroniclers of that Age found it was
Hero of Cestos. But these are all Lies: Men have
died from time to time, and Worms have eaten
them, but not for Love.

As You Like It (IV, i)

ROSALIND Men are April when they woe,
December when they wed; Maids are May when
they are Maids, but the Sky changes when they
are Wives. I will be more jealous of thee than a
Barbary Cock-pigeon over his Hen, more
clamorous than a Parrot against Rain, more
new-fangled than an Ape, more giddy in my
Desires than a Monkey. I will weep for nothing,
like Diana in the Fountain, and I will do that
when you are dispos'd to be merry; I will laugh
like a Hyen, and that when thou art inclin'd to
sleep.

As You Like It (IV, i)

CLOTEN I would this Music come. I am advised to
    give her Music a' Mornings: they say it will
    penetrate. Come on, tune. If you can penetrate
    her with your Fingering, so; we'll try with
    Tongue too. If none will do, let her remain. But
    I'll never give o'er. First, a very excellent good
    Conceited Thing; after, a wonderful sweet Air,
    with admirable rich Words to it, and then let
    her consider.

Heark, heark, the Lark at Heav'ns Gate sings,
    And Phoebus gins arise,
His Steeds to water at those Springs
        On chalic'd Flow'rs that lies;
And winking Mary-buds begin to ope their Golden Eyes
With ev'ry thing that pretty is; my Lady Sweet, arise,
        Arise, arise.

    So, get you gone. If this Penetrate, I will
    consider your Music the better

                    Cymbeline (II, iii)

KING I speak to thee plain Soldier. If thou canst
love me for this, take me. If not, to say to thee
that I shall die is true; but for thy Love, by the
Lord, no. Yet I love thee too. And while thou
liv'st, dear Kate, take a Fellow of plain and
uncoin'd Constancy, for he perforce must do
thee right, because he hath not the gift to woo
in other places. For these Fellows of infinite
Tongue, that can rime themselves into Ladies'
Favors, they do always reason themselves out
again. What, a Speaker is but a Prater, a Rime is
but a Ballad; a good Leg will fall, a straight Back
will stoop, a black Beard will turn white, a
curl'd Pate will grow bald, a fair Face will
wither, a full Eye will wax hollow; but a good
Heart, Kate, is the Sun and the Moon, or rather
the Sun and not the Moon, for it shines bright
and never changes, but keeps his Course truly. If
thou would have such a one, take me; and take
me, take a Soldier; take a Soldier, take a King.
And what say'st thou then to my Love?

Henry V (V, ii)

ARMADO I will hereupon confess I am in love; and
as it is Base for a Soldier to love, so am I in love
with a Base Wench. If drawing my Sword
against the Humour of Affection would deliver
me from the reprobate Thought of it, I would
take Desire Prisoner, and ransom him to any
French Courtier for a new devis'd Cursy. I think
scorn to sigh: me thinks I should outswear
Cupid.

Love's Labour's Lost (I, ii)

ARMADO I do affect the very Ground (which is
     base) where her Shoe (which is baser), guided
     by her Foot (which is basest), doth tread. I shall
     be forsworn (which is a great Argument of
     Falsehood) if I love. And how can that be True
     Love which is falsely attempted? Love is a
     Familiar; Love is a Divel; there is no Evil Angel
     but Love. Yet was Sampson so tempted, and he
     had an excellent Strength; yet was Salomon so
     seduced, and he had a very good Wit. Cupid's
     Buttshaft is too hard for Hercules' Club, and
     therefore too much Odds for a Spaniard's
     Rapier. The First and Second Cause will not
     serve my Turn. The Passado he respects not, the
     Duella he regards not; his Disgrace is to be
     called Boy, but his Glory is to subdue Men.
     Adieu, Valor! Rust, Rapier! Be still, Drum! For
     your Manager is in Love; yea he loveth. Assist
     me some extemporal God of Rime, for I am sure
     I shall turn Sonneter. Devise, Wit! Write, Pen!
     For I am for whole Volumes in Folio.

          Love's Labour's Lost (I, ii)

BEROWNE – Well, set thee down, Sorrow.
   – For so they say the Fool said, and
so say I, and I the Fool. – Well proved, Wit.
– By the Lord, this Love is as Mad as Aiax:
it kills Sheep, it kills me, I a Sheep. Well
proved again a' my side. I will not love. If
I do, hang me; i' faith I will not. O but her
Eye! By this Light, but for her Eye, I would
not love her; yes, for her two Eyes. Well, I
do nothing in the World but lie, and lie in my
Throat. By Heaven I do love, and it hath taught
me to Rime, and to be Mallicholy; and here is
part of my Rime, and here my Mallicholy. Well,
she hath one a' my Sonnets already: the Clown
bore it, the Fool sent it, and the Lady hath
it. Sweet Clown, sweeter Fool, sweetest Lady!
By the World,
    I would not care a Pin
    If th' other three were in.

        Love's Labour's Lost (IV, iii)

LONGAVILLE 'Did not the Heav'nly Rhet'ric of thine Eye,
'Gainst whom the World cannot hold Argument,
Persuade my Heart to this false Perjury?
Vows for thee broke deserve not Punishment.
A woman I forswore, but I will prove,
Thou being a Goddess, I forswore not thee.
My Vow was Earthly, thou a Heav'nly Love.
Thy Grace being gain'd cures all Disgrace in me.
Vows are but Breath, and Breath a Vapor is.
Then thou, fair Sun which on my Earth doost shine,
Exhal'st this Vapor-vow. In thee it is:
If broken then, it is no Fault of mine.
If by me broke, what Fool is not so Wise
To loose an Oath to win a Paradise?'

Love's Labour's Lost (IV, iii)

DUMAINE 'On a Day, alack the Day,
  Love, whose Month is ever May,
  Spied a Blossom passing Fair
  Playing in the wanton Air;
  Through the Velvet Leaves the Wind,
  All unseen, can Passage find,
  That the Lover, sick to Death,
  Wish himself the Heaven's Breath.
  "Air," quoth he, "thy Cheeks may blow;
  Air, would I might triumph so!"
  But alack my Hand is sworn
  Ne'er to pluck thee from thy Throne.
  Vow, alack, for Youth unmeet:
  Youth so apt to pluck a Sweet.
  Do not call it Sin in me
  That I am forsworn for thee,
  Thou for whom Jove would swear
  Juno but an Aethiop were,
  And deny himself for Jove,
  Turning Mortal for thy Love.'

Love's Labour's Lost (IV, iii)

BEROWNE Other slow Arts entirely keep the Brain,
  And therefore finding barrain Practicers
  Scarce shew a Harvest of their heavy Toil;
  But Love first learned in a Lady's Eyes
  Lives not alone emured in the Brain,
  But with the Motion of all Elements
  Courses as swift as Thought in ev'ry Power
  And gives to ev'ry Pow'r a double Power
  Above their Functions and their Offices.
  It adds a precious Seeing to the Eye:
  A Lover's Eyes will gaze an Eagle blind.
  A Lover's Ear will hear the lowest Sound
  When the suspicious Head of Theft is stopp'd.
  Love's Feeling is more soft and sensible
  Than are the tender Horns of Cockl'd Snails.
  Love's Tongue proves dainty, Bacchus gross in Taste.
  For Valor, is not Love a Hercules,
  Still climbing Trees in the Hesperides?
  Subtil as Sphinx, as sweet and musical
  As bright Apollo's Lute, strung with his Hair.
  And when Love speaks, the Voice of all the Gods
  Make Heaven drowsy with the Harmony.
  Never durst Poet touch a Pen to write
  Until his Ink were temp'red with Love's Sighs:
  O then his Lines would ravish Savage Ears
  And plant in Tyrants mild Humility.
  From Women's Eyes this Doctrine I derive:
  They sparkle still the right Promethean Fier,
  They are the Books, the Arts, the Academes,
  That shew, contain, and nourish all the World,
  Else none at all in ought proves Excellent.

Love's Labour's Lost (IV, iii)

ANGELO What's this? what's this? Is this her fault or mine?
The tempter or the tempted, who sins most?
Ha!
Not she; nor doth she tempt: but it is I,
That, lying by the violet in the sun,
Do as the carrion does, not as the flower,
Corrupt with virtuous season. Can it be
That modesty may more betray our sense
Than woman's lightness? Having waste ground enough,
Shall we desire to raze the sanctuary,
And pitch our evils there? O, fie, fie, fie!
What dost thou, or what art thou, Angelo?
Dost thou desire her foully for those things
That make her good? O, let her brother live!
Thieves for their robbery have authority
When judges steal themselves. What! do I love her,
That I desire to hear her speak again,
And feast upon her eyes? What is 't I dream on?
O cunning enemy, that, to catch a saint,
With saints dost bait thy hook! Most dangerous
Is that temptation that doth goad us on
To sin in loving virtue: never could the strumpet,
With all her double vigour, art and nature,
Once stir my temper; but this virtuous maid
Subdues me quite. Ever till now,
When men were fond, I smil'd and wonder'd how.

Measure for Measure (II, ii)

LORENZO The Moon shines bright. In such a Night as this,
When the sweet Wind did gently kiss the Trees,
And they did make no Noise, in such a Night
Troilus, me thinks, mounted the Troian Walls
And sigh'd his Soul toward the Grecian Tents
Where Cressid lay that Night.

JESSICA   In such a Night
Did Thisby fearfully o'er-trip the Dew
And saw the Lion's Shadow ere himself,
And ran dismay'd away.

LORENZO   In such a Night
Stood Dido with a Willow in her Hand
Upon the wild Sea-banks, and waft her Love
To come again to Carthage.

JESSICA   In such a Night
Medea gather'd the enchanted Herbs
That did renew old Aeson.

LORENZO   In such a Night
Did Jessica steal from the wealthy Jew,
And with an unthrift Love did run from Venice
As far as Belmont.

JESSICA   In such a Night
Did young Lorenzo swear he lov'd her well,
Stealing her Soul with many Vows of Faith,
And nere a true one.

LORENZO   In such a Night
Did pretty Jessica (like a little Shrow)
Slaunder her Love, and he forgave it her.

The Merchant of Venice (V, i)

LYSANDER Ay me! for aught that I could ever read,
Could ever hear by Tale or History,
The Course of True Love never did run smooth.

A Midsummer Night's Dream (I, i)

HELENA How happy some o'er othersome can be!
　　Through Athens I am thought as fair as she.
　　But what of that? Demetrius thinks not so:
　　He will not know what all but he do know.
　　And as he errs, doting on Hermia's Eyes,
　　So I, admiring of his Qualities.
　　Things Base and Vile, holding no Quantity,
　　Love can transpose to Form and Dignity.
　　Love looks not with the Eyes, but with the Mind:
　　And therefore is wing'd Cupid painted Blind.
　　Nor hath Love's Mind of any Judgement taste:
　　Wings and no Eyes figure unheedy Haste.
　　And therefore is Love said to be a Child:
　　Because in Choice he is so oft beguil'd.
　　As waggish Boys in game themselves forswear,
　　So the boy Love is perjur'd every where.

A Midsummer Night's Dream (I, i)

OBERON But I might see young Cupid's fiery Shaft
        Quench'd in the chast Beams of the wat'ry Moon,
        And the imperial Vot'ress passed on
        In Maiden Meditation, Fancy-free.
        Yet mark'd I where the Bolt of Cupid fell:
        It fell upon a little Western Flower,
        Before Milk-white, now Purple with Love's Wound,
        And Maidens call it Love-in-Idleness.

        A Midsummer Night's Dream (II, i)

THISBY Asleep, my Love?
  What, dead, my Dove?
O Pyramus arise;
  Speak, speak. Quite dumbe?
  Dead, dead? A Tumbe
Must cover thy sweet Eyes.
  These lily Lips,
  This cherry Nose,
These yellow cowslip Cheeks,
  Are gone, are gone:
  Lovers, make moan.
His Eyes were green as Leeks.
  O Sisters Three,
  Come, come to me
With Hands as pale as Milk;
  Lay them in Gore,
  Since you have shore
With Shears his Threed of Silk.
  Tongue, not a Word:
  Come, trusty Sword,
Come Blade, my Breast imbrew: *[Stabs herself]*
  And farewell, Friends:
  Thus Thisby ends.
Adieu, adieu, adieu.   *[Dies]*

A Midsummer Night's Dream (V, i)

OTHELLO   I did consent,
   And often did beguile her of her Tears
   When I did speak of some distressful Stroke
   That my Youth suffer'd. My Story being done,
   She gave me for my Pains a World of Kisses:
   She swore in faith 'twas strange, 'twas passing strange,
   'Twas pitiful, 'twas wondrous pitiful.
   She wish'd she had not heard it, yet she wish'd
   That Heaven had made her such a Man. She thank'd me,
   And bad me, if I had a Friend that lov'd her,
   I should teach him how to tell my Story,
   And that would woo her. Upon this Hint I spake:
   She lov'd me for the Dangers I had past,
   And I lov'd her that she did pity them.
   This onely is the Witchcraft I have us'd.

                    Othello (I, iii)

ROMEO Love is a Smoke made with the Fume of Sighs;
Being purg'd, a Fire sparkling in Lovers' Eyes;
Being vex'd, a Sea nourish'd with Loving Tears.
What is it else? A Madness most discreet,
A choking Gall, and a preserving Sweet.

Romeo and Juliet (I, i)

ROMEO   O she doth teach the Torches to burn bright.
   It seems she hangs upon the Cheek of Night
   As a rich Jewel in an Ethiop's Ear:
   Beauty too rich for Use, for Earth too dear.
   So shows a snowy Dove trooping with Crows
   As yonder Lady o'er her Fellows shows.
   The Measure done, I'll watch her place of Stand,
   And, touching hers, make blessed my rude Hand.
   Did my Heart love till now? Forswear it, Sight;
   For I ne'er saw true Beauty till this Night.

Romeo and Juliet (I, iv)

ROMEO − But soft, what Light through yonder Window breaks?
It is the East, and Juliet is the Sun.
Arise, fair Sun, and kill the envious Moon,
Who is already sick and pale with Grief
That thou her Maid art far more fair than she.
Be not her Maid, since she is envious:
Her Vestal Livery is but sick and green,
And none but Fools do wear it. Cast it off.
It is my Lady, O it is my Love:
O that she knew she were.
She speaks, yet she says nothing: what of that?
Her Eye discourses; I will answer it.
I am too bold: 'tis not to me she speaks.
Two of the fairest Stars in all Heaven,
Having some Business, do entreat her Eyes
To twinkle in their Spheres till they return.
What if her Eyes were there, they in her Head?
The brightness of her Cheek would shame those Stars
As Day-light doth a Lamp; her Eyes in Heaven
Would through the Airy Region stream so bright
That Birds would sing and think it were not Night.
See how she leans her Cheek upon her Hand:
O that I were a Glove upon that Hand,
That I might touch that Cheek.

Romeo and Juliet (II, i)

JULIET   My Bounty is as boundless as the Sea,
My Love as deep; the more I give to thee
The more I have, for both are infinite.

Romeo and Juliet (II, i)

JULIET   Gallop apace, you fiery footed Steeds,
    Towards Phoebus' Lodging. Such a Wagoner
    As Phaeton would whip you to the West
    And bring in cloudy Night immediately.
    Spread thy close Curtain, Love-performing Night,
    That Runaways' Eyes may wink, and Romeo
    Leap to these Arms untalk'd of and unseen.
    Lovers can see to do their amorous Rights,
    And by their own Beauties; or, if Love be blind,
    It best agrees with Night. Come, civil Night,
    Thou sober-suited Matron all in black,
    And learn me how to loose a winning Match
    Play'd for a pair of stainless Maidenhoods.
    Hood my unmann'd Blood, bating in my Cheeks,
    With thy black Mantle till strange Love grow bold,
    Think True-love acted simple Modesty.
    Come Night, come Romeo, come thou Day in Night,
    For thou wilt lie upon the Wings of Night
    Whiter than new Snow upon a Raven's Back.
    Come gentle Night, come loving, black-brow'd Night,
    Give me my Romeo, and when I shall die,
    Take him and cut him out in little Stars,
    And he will make the Face of Heaven so fine
    That all the World will be in love with Night
    And pay no Worship to the garish Sun.
    O I have bought the Mansion of a Love
    But not possess'd it; and though I am sold,
    Not yet enjoy'd. So tedious is this Day
    As is the Night before some Festival
    To an impatient Child that hath new Robes
    And may not wear them.

                        Romeo and Juliet (III. ii)

PETRUCHIO – Good morrow, Kate, for that's your Name, I hear.

KATHERINA Well have you heard, but something hard of
    Hearing:
They call me Kath'rine that do talk of me.

PETRUCHIO You lie, in faith, for you are call'd Plain Kate,
And Bonny Kate, and sometimes Kate the Curst.
But Kate, the prettiest Kate in Christendom,
Kate of Kate Hall, my Super-Dainty Kate,
For Dainties all are Kates, and therefore, Kate,
Take this of me, Kate of my Consolation:
Hearing thy Mildness prais'd in every Town,
Thy Virtues spoke of, and thy Beauty sounded,
Yet not so deeply as to thee belongs,
My self am mov'd to woo thee for my Wife.

KATHERINA Mov'd! In good time let him that mov'd you hither
Remove you hence! I knew you at the first
You were a Movable.

PETRUCHIO   Why, what's a Movable?

KATHERINA A Join'd Stool.

PETRUCHIO   Thou hast hit 't: come sit on me.

KATHERINA Asses are made to bear, and so are you.

PETRUCHIO Women are made to bear, and so are you.

*　*　*

Thus in Plain Terms: your Father hath consented
That you shall be my Wife, your Dowry 'greed on,
And will you, nill you, I will marry you.
Now Kate, I am a Husband for your Turn,
For by this Light whereby I see thy Beauty,
Thy Beauty that doth make me like thee well,
Thou must be marri'd to no Man but me.
For I am he am born to tame you, Kate,
And bring you from a Wild Kate to a Kate
Comfortable as other Household Kates.
Here comes your Father. Never make denial:
I must and will have Kath'rine to my Wife.

*　*　*

And to conclude, we've 'greed so well together
That upon Sunday is the Wedding Day.
KATHERINA   I'll see thee hang'd on Sunday first!

The Taming of the Shrew (II, i)

DUKE   If Music be the Food of Love, play on,
        Give me Excess of it: that, surfeiting,
        The Appetite may sicken, and so die.
        That Strain again, it had a dying Fall:
        O, it came o'er my Ear like the sweet Sound
        That breathes upon a Bank of Violets,
        Stealing, and giving Odour. Enough, no more,
        'Tis not so Sweet now as it was before.
        – O spirit of Love, how quick and fresh art thou,
        That notwithstanding thy Capacity,
        Receiveth as the Sea. Nought enters there,
        Of what Validity and Pitch so ere,
        But falls into Abatement and Low Price
        Even in a Minute. So full of Shapes is Fancy
        That it alone is high Fantastical.

                    Twelfth Night (I, i)

VIOLA   My Father had a Daughter lov'd a Man
    As it might be, perhaps, were I a Woman,
    I should your Lordship.
DUKE   And what's her History?
VIOLA   A Blank, my Lord: she never told her Love,
    But let Concealment like a Worm i'th' Bud
    Feed on her Damask Cheek: she pin'd in Thought,
    And with a green and yellow Melancholy
    She sate like Patience on a Monument,
    Smiling at Grief. Was not this Love indeed?
    We Men may say more, swear more, but indeed
    Our Shews are more than Will: for still we prove
    Much in our Vows, but little in our Love.

                    Twelfth Night (II, iv)

VALENTINE To be in love, where Scorn is bought with Groans;
    Coy Looks with Heart-sore Sighs; one fading moment's Mirth
    With twenty watchful, weary, tedious Nights;
    If hap'ly won, perhaps a hapless Gain;
    If lost, why then a grievous Labor won.
    How ever, but a Folly bought with Wit,
    Or else a Wit by Folly vanquished.

               The Two Gentlemen of Verona (I, i)

VALENTINE I have done Penance for contemning Love,
Whose high imperious thoughts have punish'd me
With bitter Fasts, with penitential Groans,
With nightly Tears, and daily Heart-sore Sighs:
For in revenge of my contempt of Love,
Love hath chas'd Sleep from my enthralled Eyes
And made them Watchers of mine own Heart's Sorrow.
O gentle Protheus, Love's a mighty Lord,
And hath so humbled me, as I confess
There is no Woe to his Correction;
Nor, to his Service, no such Joy on Earth;
Now no Discourse except it be of Love;
Now can I break my fast, dine, sup, and sleep
Upon the very naked name of Love.

The Two Gentlemen of Verona (II, iv)

DUKE 'My Thoughts do harbor with my Silvia nightly,
       And Slaves they are to me that send them flying.
       O, could their Master come and go as lightly,
       Himself would lodge where, senseless, they are lying.
       My Herald Thoughts, in thy pure Bosom rest them,
       While I, their King, that thither them importune
       Do curse the Grace that with such Grace hath blest them,
       Because my Self do want my Servants' Fortune.
           I curse my Self, for they are sent by me,
           That they should harbor where their Lord should be.
           Silvia, this Night I will enfranchise thee.'

                    The Two Gentlemen of Verona (III, i)

VALENTINE   And why not Death rather than living Torment?
    To die is to be banish'd from my Self,
    And Silvia is my Self: banish'd from her
    Is Self from Self, a deadly Banishment.
    What Light is Light if Silvia be not seen?
    What Joy is Joy if Silvia be not by?
    Unless it be to think that she is by,
    And feed upon the Shadow of Perfection.
    Except I be by Silvia in the Night,
    There is no Music in the Nightingale.
    Unless I look on Silvia in the Day,
    There is no Day for me to look upon.
    She is my Essence, and I leave to be
    If I be not by her fair Influence
    Foster'd, illumin'd, cherish'd, kept alive.
    I fly not Death to fly his deadly Doom;
    Tarry I here, I but attend on Death,
    But fly I hence, I fly away from Life.

The Two Gentlemen of Verona (III, i)

Sometime she shakes her Head, and then his Hand;
Now gazeth she on him, now on the Ground;
Sometime her Arms enfold him like a Band.
She would, he will not in her Arms be bound;
    And when from thence he struggles to be gone,
    She locks her Lily Fingers one in one.

'Fondling,' she saith, 'Since I have hemm'd thee here
Within the Circuit of this Iv'ry Pale,
I'll be a Park, and thou shalt be my Deer.
Feed where thou wilt, on Mountain or in Dale;
    Graze on my Lips, and if those Hills be dry
    Stray lower, where the pleasant Fountains lie.

'Within this Limit is Relief enough,
Sweet Bottom Grass, and high delightful Plain,
Round rising Hillocks, Brakes obscure and rough,
To shelter thee from Tempest and from Rain.
    Then be my Deer, since I am such a Park;
    No Dog shall rouse thee, though a thousand bark.'

Venus and Adonis

Index

The Sonnets

Songs from the Plays

The Plays

Acknowledgements

The Globe Theatre, detail from an engraving, 1616 by Cornelius de Visscher
British Library, London/Bridgeman Art Library, London/New York

Ophelia by John William Waterhouse (1849–1917)
Christie's Images, London/Bridgeman Art Library, London/New York

Romeo and Juliet, 1876 (pen & ink and black chalk) by Ford Madox Brown (1821–93)
Bradford Art Galleries and Museums/Bridgeman Art Library, London/New York

Title Page with a portrait of Shakespeare, from *Mr William Shakespeare's Comedies, Histories and Tragedies*, edited by J. Heminge and H. Condell, engraving by Droeshurt, 1623
British Library, London/Bridgeman Art Library, London/New York

Everyman's Poetry

Titles available in this series

Matthew Arnold
0 460 87961 8

Jane Austen
0 460 87959 6

William Blake
0 460 87800 X

The Brontës
0 460 87864 6

Rupert Brooke &
Wilfred Owen
0 460 87801 8

Elizabeth Barrett
Browning
0 460 87894 8

Charles Baudelaire
0 460 87993 6

Robert Browning
0 460 87893 X

Robert Burns
0 460 87814 X

Lord Byron
0 460 87810 7

Geoffrey Chaucer:
Comic and Bawdy Tales
0 460 87869 7

Geoffrey Chaucer:
Three Tales About
Marriage
0 460 87870 0

John Clare
0 460 87823 9

Arthur Hugh Clough
0 460 87939 1

Samuel Taylor Coleridge
0 460 87826 3

William Cowper
0 460 87991 X

Dante
0 460 87955 3

Emily Dickinson
0 460 87895 6

John Donne
0 460 87901 4

John Dryden
0 460 87940 5

English Sonnets
0 460 87990 1

Evergreen Verse
0 460 87666 9

Four Metaphysical Poets
0 460 87857 3

Oliver Goldsmith
0 460 87827 1

Thomas Gray
0 460 87805 0

Ivor Gurney
0 460 87797 6

Thomas Hardy
0 460 87956 1

Heinrich Heine
0 460 87865 4

George Herbert
0 460 87795 X

Robert Herrick
0 460 87799 2

Homer
0 460 87997 9

John Keats
0 460 87808 5

Omar Khayyám
0 460 87954 5

Rudyard Kipling
0 460 87941 3

D.H. Lawrence
0 460 87962 6